# Cool Calendar Skills, Grades K–1

## Contents

## Introduction

Learning about days, weeks, months, and years is an abstract concept and can be difficult for young children to understand. The daily use of the calendar provides many opportunities to teach time measurement as well as other math concepts such as recognizing numbers, counting, and patterning. The ideas in this book are designed to provide the teacher with games, songs, and various activities that will help young children, regardless of their learning style, develop these concepts. Any activity may be adapted or modified to best meet the needs of individual children.

The first part of this book provides the teacher with ideas on how to involve children in the preparation of the class calendar each month. It also has several ideas for each month that provide practice learning calendar skills plus additional math skills.

The Calendar Readiness unit includes activities on sequencing events, learning about seasons, days of the week, months of the year, and the basic use of a calendar. These activities can be used as an introduction or as a review, depending on the children's abilities.

The Monthly Calendar Activities unit includes a calendar activity for each month of the year. In addition, there are two activities per month that provide practice on seasons, holidays, and themes. These pages are reproducible and are meant to be copied for individual use.

# BASIC USE OF THE CALENDAR IN THE CLASSROOM

## Classroom Calendar Setup

The use of the calendar in the classroom can provide children with daily practice on learning days, weeks, months, and years. As you plan the setup for your classroom, include enough space on the wall to staple a calendar grid labeled with the days of the week. Leave space above the grid for the name of the month and the year. Next to the calendar, staple twelve cards labeled with the months of the year and the number of days in each month. Leave these items on the wall all year. At the beginning of each month, start with the blank calendar grid. Do not staple anything on the grid that refers to the new month. Leave the days of the week and the year in place.

## Calendar Basket for First Day of Each Month

Before the children arrive, gather all of the items that will go on the new calendar. You may want to include the name of the month, number cards, cards to indicate birthdays during the month, and cards that tell about special holidays or school events during the month. You may also wish to wrap a small treat such as sugarless gum which can be taped on the day of each child's birthday. Add a special pointer that can be used each day while doing calendar activities. See Teacher Ideas on pages 3 through 6. Place these items in a picnic basket. Select a puppet that can remain in the basket and come out only to bring items for each new month. A dog puppet works well because of the large mouth which makes it easier to grasp each item.

Place the picnic basket in front of the class. Pull out the puppet and introduce it to the children. Explain that the puppet will visit on the first day of each month to bring the new calendar items. Then have the puppet pull out the name of the month. According to the abilities of your children, have them name the first letter in the name of the month, count the letters, or find the vowels. Staple the name of the month above the calendar. Have the puppet pull out the new pointer for the helper to use each day during calendar time.

Next, pull out the number cards for the month. You may use plain number cards, or you may want to use seasonal die-cut shapes. By using two or three die-cut shapes, you can incorporate building patterns as part of your daily calendar routine. See pages 3 through 6 for pattern ideas. Place the number one card or die-cut under the day of the week on which the new month begins. Locate the new month on the month cards stapled next to your calendar. Have the children tell how many days this month will have and have them count that many spaces on the calendar to indicate the end of the month. You may wish to place a small stop sign as a visual reminder of the end of the month. Save the remaining number cards or die-cut shapes and add one each day.

If there are any birthdays during the new month, have the puppet pull out of the basket the cards that have a birthday symbol with the child's name and birth date written on it. Count from the number 1 to find where to staple this as a visual reminder of each child's birthday. If you have included a wrapped treat for each child, tape it on the calendar on the correct day.

Finally, have the puppet bring out cards that have pictures of holidays or special happenings, such as field trips, picture day, or story time in the library. Staple the picture cards on the correct day on the calendar grid. You can use these to practice various counting skills such as counting how many days until a field trip, a birthday, or a holiday. When the basket is empty, say goodbye to the puppet and return it to the picnic basket. Put the basket away until the next month. The children will look forward to the beginning of each new month in order to see what items the puppet will bring for the class calendar.

## AUGUST

☼ **Pointer**   Include a fish pointer in the calendar basket (see page 2) for this month. To make a pointer, you will need two 3" fish shapes cut from poster board, a medium-sized dowel rod that is 18" long, and several 12" lengths of narrow blue and yellow ribbon. Hot-glue the ribbons to the end of the dowel rod so that they lay against the rod. Then hot-glue the two fish shapes to the end of the dowel rod so that the fish covers the glued ends of the ribbons. The calendar helper can use this to point to the day of the week, the number, the month, and the year as the class says the date each day.

☼ **Sequencing**   Help children begin to understand the concept of yesterday, today, and tomorrow by blowing up a small balloon and tying it. Staple the tied end to the current day of the month. Tell the children that the balloon shows which day on the calendar represents today. When the children look at the calendar the next day, tell them that the day with the balloon on it is now yesterday. Since that day is over, pop the balloon to indicate that yesterday is gone. Blow up a new balloon, staple it to the calendar, and repeat the activity. Continue this procedure as long as the children show interest.

☼ **Song**   Sing the following song for children to learn the days of the week:

*(Tune: "Here We Go Round the Mulberry Bush")*
Seven days in every week,
every week, every week.
Seven days in every week.
Let's say them all.
Sunday, Monday,
Tuesday, Wednesday,
Thursday, Friday, Saturday.  (Repeat)

## SEPTEMBER

☼ **Pointer**   Include an apple pointer in the calendar basket for this month. To make a pointer, follow the directions given in August. Replace the fish shape with an apple shape and use red and yellow ribbons.

☼ **Patterning**   Practice the concept of patterning by writing the numbers 1–30 on two die-cut shapes, such as a fall leaf and an apple. Write the numbers on the shapes in order using an ABABAB pattern. After the first few days, ask the children if they notice anything special about the shapes on the calendar. Younger children may not understand patterning yet but will become more aware as the pattern develops. Use this as a review for older children.

## SEPTEMBER - *continued*

☼ **Song**   Have children sing the following song to learn the months of the year:

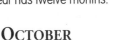

*(Tune: "Clementine")*
Every year has twelve months,
Every year has twelve months.
January, February,
March, April, and May.
June, July, and August,
September and October,
November and December,
Every year has twelve months.

## OCTOBER

☼ **Pointer**   Include a spider pointer in the calendar basket for this month. You will need two 2" black pompoms, four black chenille stems, a medium-sized dowel rod that is 18" long, several 12" lengths of narrow black and orange ribbon, and a piece of fine wire. Hot-glue the ribbons to the end of the dowel rod so that they lay against the rod. Then hot-glue the two pompoms together to make the spider's body. Cut the chenille stems in half and hot-glue them to one side of the pompoms. Bend the stems to look like eight legs. Tie the spider to the end of the dowel rod with a piece of fine wire.

☼ **Patterning**   Practice patterning by writing the numbers 1–31 on two different die-cut shapes, such as a bat and a pumpkin. Write the numbers on the shapes in order using an AABBAABB pattern. Extend this activity by having children color the pattern on their own October calendar on page 33.

☼ **Graphing**   Practice graphing by stapling a large piece of white paper on the wall and drawing three columns. At the top of the columns, draw three pumpkins with the following faces: happy, scary, and mad. Give each child one fourth of a sheet of white construction paper and have them draw the kind of face they like best. Then have them glue their pumpkin drawing on the graph below the face that they chose. Use this graph to decide what kind of face to carve on the class pumpkin.

## NOVEMBER

☼ **Pointer**   Include a turkey pointer in the calendar basket for this month. To make a pointer, follow the directions given in August. Replace the fish shape with a turkey shape and use brown and orange ribbons.

☼ **Patterning**   Practice patterning by writing the numbers 1–30 on three different die-cut shapes, such as a turkey, Pilgrim boy hat, and a Pilgrim girl hat. Write the numbers on the shapes in order using an ABCABC pattern. At the end of the month, challenge the children to find the diagonal pattern that has also developed.

☼ **Months**   Have children play "Who's Missing?" On twelve pieces of construction paper, write the months of the year. Select twelve children and have them line up in front of the class. Give each child a month starting with January and have them hold it up so that the months can be seen. Ask the rest of the children to close their eyes. The teacher will silently pick one child to go hide. Then ask children to open their eyes and guess which month is missing. To increase the level of difficulty, pass out the months in mixed-up order.

## DECEMBER

☼ **Pointer**   Include a candle pointer in the calendar basket for this month. To make a pointer, follow the directions given in August. Replace the fish shape with a candle shape and use red and green ribbons. You may wish to cover the candle shapes with gold glitter.

☼ **Counting Down**   For the number cards this month, you may want to use red tree cutouts and green tree cutouts. Glue one red tree to one green tree. Write the numbers 1–31 on the green side. Count how many days until winter break begins. For example, the last school day before winter break may be December 20. On the back of the green tree on which the number 1 is written, write number 20; on number 2 write 19; on number 3 write 18, and so on. On the first day of the month, place all of the green trees on the calendar in order. Each day the calendar helper will turn over the green tree to see the red tree. The numbers on the red tree will go in reverse so that the children can count down to the last day before winter break.

## DECEMBER - *continued*

☼ **Graphing**   Use the class birthday chart to practice graphing. First, have children fold a large piece of construction paper into four columns and write the names of the four seasons at the bottom of the columns. Look at the birthday chart to find the names of children who have birthdays during each season. Write the names in the appropriate column. Discuss which seasons have the fewest and the most birthdays. For younger children, you may want to do this activity on a large class graph.

## JANUARY

☼ **Pointer**   Include a glove pointer in the calendar basket for this month. To make a pointer, you will need one knitted glove (any color), some narrow ribbon, a small amount of polyester fiberfill, and a medium-sized dowel rod that is 18" long. Stuff the glove with the fiberfill until it takes the shape of a hand. Bend the thumb and fingers down, leaving the pointer finger extended, and stitch in place. Cover the end of the dowel rod with hot glue and insert it into the glove. Secure the glove to the rod by tying the ribbon around the wrist.

☼ **Patterning**   Practice patterning by writing the numbers 1–31 on three die-cut shapes, such as a snowman, a mitten, and a snowman's hat. Place the shapes in order using an ABBCABBC pattern. As the children add a shape for each day of the month, they will begin to see the pattern develop. Challenge them to predict the shape for specific days. For example, what will the shape be on the last Thursday of the month or on a child's birthday?

☼ **Reinforcing Patterning**   Select plastic cubes that coordinate with the colors of the shapes on the calendar. For example, use a white plastic cube to represent the snowman shape, a red plastic cube for the mitten, and a black plastic cube for the snowman's hat. As the calendar helper adds a shape to the calendar each day, also have him/her snap together a plastic cube of the same color. Place the plastic cube train on a shelf or ledge below the calendar so that the children will be able to see the pattern develop.

## FEBRUARY

☼ **Pointer**   Include a heart pointer in the calendar basket for this month. To make a pointer, follow the directions given in August. Replace the fish shape with a heart shape and use red and white ribbons. You may wish to cover the hearts with red glitter.

☼ **Patterning**   Practice patterning by writing the numbers 1–28 (29 in a leap year) on red, pink, and white heart shapes, in that order. On the back of all the red hearts write "I," and on the back of all the white hearts, write "U." Leave all the pink hearts blank. For the month of February, place all hearts on the calendar at the beginning of the month, making sure that the numbers are showing. After saying the date for the day, the calendar helper will turn the heart over to reveal part of the secret message. The children will soon recognize the message: I♥U. The message will be repeated several times throughout the month.

☼ **Song**   Have children learn the following song about Mr. Groundhog:

*(Tune: "Frere Jacques")*
Mr. Groundhog, Mr. Groundhog,
time to wake up, time to wake up.
If you see your shadow, if you see your shadow,
Winter stays, go back to sleep.

Mr. Groundhog, Mr. Groundhog,
time to wake up, time to wake up.
If you see no shadow, if you see no shadow,
Spring is near, stay out and play.

## MARCH

☼ **Pointer**   Include a shamrock pointer in the calendar basket for this month. To make a pointer, follow the directions given in August. Replace the fish shape with a shamrock shape and use green and yellow ribbons. You may wish to cover the shamrocks with green glitter.

☼ **Patterning**   Practice patterning by writing the numbers 1–31 on die-cut shapes. You may want to use kite shapes in four different colors, such as green, yellow, orange, and purple. Write the numbers on the kite shapes in order using an ABCDABCD pattern. Have the children predict what color the kite will be on various days, such as the last day of the month.

☼ **Floor Calendar**   Have the children use a floor calendar to practice calendar skills. With a permanent marker, draw a large calendar grid on a rectangular-shaped piece of paper or a plastic tablecloth. Write the days of the week across the top of the grid and write the numbers on the calendar matching the current month. Place the grid on the floor and have children sit around it so that they all can see. Call on one child at a time to show the answer to various questions by standing on the correct date. Directions may include asking the child to stand on a special day during the month, on his/her birthday, or the second Saturday. Vary the difficulty according to the children's abilities.

## APRIL

☼ **Pointer**   Include a butterfly pointer in the calendar basket for this month. To make a pointer, follow the directions given in August. Replace the fish shape with a butterfly shape and use pink and yellow ribbons. Or, you can use a plastic butterfly in place of a butterfly shape.

☼ **Patterning**   Practice patterning by writing the numbers 1–30 on three die-cut shapes, such as a raindrop, an umbrella, and a cloud. Write the numbers on the shapes in order using an ABACABAC pattern. After the pattern has been repeated several times on the calendar, challenge children to think of other ways to make the same pattern. For example, the children might write numbers to replace the raindrop, umbrella, and cloud to make a 12131213 pattern.

☼ **Estimation**   Practice estimation by having the children predict how many rainy days there will be in April. At the beginning of the month, write their predictions on a piece of paper and staple it next to the calendar. On the last day of the month, count the rainy days during April and refer back to the children's predictions to see whose estimation was the closest to the correct number.

## MAY

☼ **Pointer**   Include a flower pointer in the calendar basket for this month. To make a pointer, follow the directions given in August. Replace the fish shape with a flower shape and use purple and pink ribbons. You may wish to use a silk flower in place of a flower shape.

☼ **Patterning**   Practice patterning by writing the numbers 1–31 on two die-cut shapes, such as a flower and a butterfly. Write the numbers on the shapes in order using a growing pattern such as ABAABBAAABBB. After the pattern has been repeated a few times, assign body movements to the flower and butterfly. For example, clap each time there is a flower on the calendar and snap for the butterfly. Have children act out the pattern with body movements.

☼ **Calendar Bingo**   Review calendar skills by making for each child a copy of the May calendar on page 54. Give them several small items to use as markers. You may use candies or crackers that can be eaten after the activity is completed. Call out various days of the week and dates of the month and have children cover them with their markers. Vary difficulty according to the abilities of the children.

## JUNE

☼ **Pointer**   Include a sun pointer in the calendar basket for this month. To make a pointer, follow the directions given in August. Replace the fish shape with a sun shape and use gold and yellow ribbons. You may wish to cover the sun with gold glitter.

☼ **Secret Message**   Write the numbers for this month's calendar on letter die-cuts and glue the letters onto white squares. Have the letters spell a special message such as *Goodbye* or *I'll Miss You*. The number of letters in the message should equal the number of days of school during June. Be sure to include Saturdays and Sundays. As the calendar helper adds a number to the calendar each day, the secret message will be revealed.

## JUNE - *continued*

☼ **Writing Dates**   Have the children create a sentence about something they are planning to do during the summer break. Ask them to imagine on what day of the week this might happen and include it in their sentence. For older children, encourage them to imagine the day of the week and the date. For example, "I will go swimming on Saturday, June 11."

## JULY

☼ **Pointer**   Include a star pointer in the calendar basket for this month. To make a pointer, follow the directions given in August. Replace the fish shape with a star shape and use red, white, and blue ribbons. You may wish to cover the star with silver glitter.

☼ **Flag Pattern**   Use red, white, and blue squares for the July calendar numbers. Add a white star to the blue squares. Before writing the numbers on the squares, arrange the colors so that the blue squares with stars are placed under Sunday, Monday, and Tuesday for the first two weeks. The remaining squares should be placed so that the first week is red, the second week is white, and so on. Make a few extra blue and red squares with no numbers to fill in the blank boxes on the calendar grid. Before writing the numbers 1–31 on the cards, arrange all of the colored squares to resemble the flag. Look at a current calendar to find out on which day of the week the month begins and write the first number so that it corresponds with that day. Continue writing numbers on the remaining squares, keeping in mind that there may be blank squares before number 1 and after 31. The calendar helper will add a square each day, and the flag will be revealed.

☼ **Similarities**   Have children design their own flag. Then have them look at all of the flags and use their sorting skills to find similar attributes. Ask them to decide which flags have the same attributes and can be grouped together. Encourage children to name the attributes.

# Sequence Three Events

**1.**

**2.**

**3.**

Have children write numbers to show what happens first, next, and last.

**7**

**Unit 1: Calendar Readiness**
Cool Calendar Skills K-1, SV 7099-8

# Sequence Four Events

**1.**

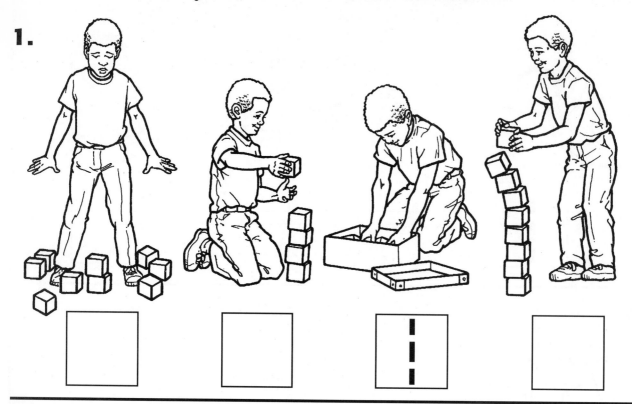

**2.**

Have children write numbers to show the order in which the events happen.

# Draw Events in Order

Morning

Afternoon

Night

Have children draw something that they would do at each time of day.

# Seasons

### Fall

### Winter

### Spring

### Summer

Have children cut out the pictures. Then, ask them to glue each picture in the box next to the season where it belongs.

Name _____     Date _____

# Seasons: Special Days in Spring

| March | April | May |
|-------|-------|-----|
|       |       |     |

Discuss with children St. Patrick's Day, Earth Day, and Mother's Day. Have children find the picture of the special day that happens in each month. Ask them to cut out and glue the pictures in the boxes.

# Seasons: Special Days in Summer

| June | July | August |
|------|------|--------|
|      |      |        |

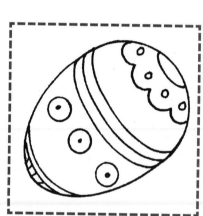

Discuss with children Father's Day, Fourth of July, and Watermelon Day. Have children find the picture of the special day that happens in each month. Ask them to cut out and glue the pictures in the boxes.

# Seasons: Special Days in Fall

## September      October      November

Discuss with children Grandparent's Day, Columbus Day, and Thanksgiving. Have children find the picture of the special day that happens in each month. Ask them to cut out and glue the pictures in the boxes.

Name _____   Date _____

# Seasons: Special Days in Winter

| December | January | February |
|---|---|---|

Discuss with children Christmas, New Year's Day, and Valentine's Day. Have children find the picture of the special day that happens in each month. Ask them to cut out and glue the pictures in the boxes.

**Unit 1: Calendar Readiness**
Cool Calendar Skills K-1, SV 7099-8

# Days of the Week

| | |
|---|---|
| Tuesday | Friday |
| Monday | Wednesday |
| Thursday | Sunday |
| Saturday | **The Days of the Week** |

Have children learn the "Days of the Week" song on page 3. Ask them to cut out the days of the week cards and arrange them in order. You may wish to have children make a book by stapling the pages together.

# More Days of the Week

1. Sunday

2. Monday

3. Tuesday

4. Wednesday

5. Thursday

6. Friday

7. Saturday

Have children draw a line from each day of the week to the object that starts with the same beginning sound.

Name _____  Date _____

# Favorite Day of the Week

My favorite day of the week is _____.

I like to _____.

---

Discuss with children the day of the week that is your favorite. Have children write their favorite day and write what they like to do on that day. Ask them to draw a picture showing what they like to do.

# Order the Days of the Week

## February

| Sunday | Monday | Tuesday | Wednesday | Thursday | Friday | Saturday |
|--------|--------|---------|-----------|----------|--------|----------|
|  | 1 | 2 | 3 | 4 | 5 | 6 |
| 7 | 8 | 9 | 10 | 11 | 12 | 13 |
| 14 | 15 | 16 | 17 | 18 | 19 | 20 |
| 21 | 22 | 23 | 24 | 25 | 26 | 27 |
| 28 |  |  |  |  |  |  |

Have children write the days of the week in order. Ask them to color the Tuesdays blue.

# Months of the Year

| | | |
|---|---|---|
| **June** | **April** | **September** |
| **February** | **October** | **January** |
| **December** | **March** | **July** |
| **August** | **May** | **November** |

Discuss with children the months of the year. Ask them to cut out the months of the year cards and arrange them in order. You may wish to call out children's birthdays and have them hold up the correct month.

# Ordering the Months of the Year

### January

| S | M | T | W | T | F | S |
|---|---|---|---|---|---|---|
|   |   |   |   |   | 1 | 2 |
| 3 | 4 | 5 | 6 | 7 | 8 | 9 |
| 10 | 11 | 12 | 13 | 14 | 15 | 16 |
| 17 | 18 | 19 | 20 | 21 | 22 | 23 |
| 24 31 | 25 | 26 | 27 | 28 | 29 | 30 |

### February

| S | M | T | W | T | F | S |
|---|---|---|---|---|---|---|
|   | 1 | 2 | 3 | 4 | 5 | 6 |
| 7 | 8 | 9 | 10 | 11 | 12 | 13 |
| 14 | 15 | 16 | 17 | 18 | 19 | 20 |
| 21 | 22 | 23 | 24 | 25 | 26 | 27 |
| 28 |   |   |   |   |   |   |

### March

| S | M | T | W | T | F | S |
|---|---|---|---|---|---|---|
|   | 1 | 2 | 3 | 4 | 5 | 6 |
| 7 | 8 | 9 | 10 | 11 | 12 | 13 |
| 14 | 15 | 16 | 17 | 18 | 19 | 20 |
| 21 | 22 | 23 | 24 | 25 | 26 | 27 |
| 28 | 29 | 30 | 31 |   |   |   |

### April

| S | M | T | W | T | F | S |
|---|---|---|---|---|---|---|
|   |   |   |   | 1 | 2 | 3 |
| 4 | 5 | 6 | 7 | 8 | 9 | 10 |
| 11 | 12 | 13 | 14 | 15 | 16 | 17 |
| 18 | 19 | 20 | 21 | 22 | 23 | 24 |
| 25 | 26 | 27 | 28 | 29 | 30 |   |

### May

| S | M | T | W | T | F | S |
|---|---|---|---|---|---|---|
|   |   |   |   |   |   | 1 |
| 2 | 3 | 4 | 5 | 6 | 7 | 8 |
| 9 | 10 | 11 | 12 | 13 | 14 | 15 |
| 16 | 17 | 18 | 19 | 20 | 21 | 22 |
| 23 30 | 24 31 | 25 | 26 | 27 | 28 | 29 |

### June

| S | M | T | W | T | F | S |
|---|---|---|---|---|---|---|
|   |   | 1 | 2 | 3 | 4 | 5 |
| 6 | 7 | 8 | 9 | 10 | 11 | 12 |
| 13 | 14 | 15 | 16 | 17 | 18 | 19 |
| 20 | 21 | 22 | 23 | 24 | 25 | 26 |
| 27 | 28 | 29 | 30 |   |   |   |

### July

| S | M | T | W | T | F | S |
|---|---|---|---|---|---|---|
|   |   |   |   | 1 | 2 | 3 |
| 4 | 5 | 6 | 7 | 8 | 9 | 10 |
| 11 | 12 | 13 | 14 | 15 | 16 | 17 |
| 18 | 19 | 20 | 21 | 22 | 23 | 24 |
| 25 | 26 | 27 | 28 | 29 | 30 | 31 |

### August

| S | M | T | W | T | F | S |
|---|---|---|---|---|---|---|
| 1 | 2 | 3 | 4 | 5 | 6 | 7 |
| 8 | 9 | 10 | 11 | 12 | 13 | 14 |
| 15 | 16 | 17 | 18 | 19 | 20 | 21 |
| 22 | 23 | 24 | 25 | 26 | 27 | 28 |
| 29 | 30 | 31 |   |   |   |   |

### September

| S | M | T | W | T | F | S |
|---|---|---|---|---|---|---|
|   |   |   | 1 | 2 | 3 | 4 |
| 5 | 6 | 7 | 8 | 9 | 10 | 11 |
| 12 | 13 | 14 | 15 | 16 | 17 | 18 |
| 19 | 20 | 21 | 22 | 23 | 24 | 25 |
| 26 | 27 | 28 | 29 | 30 |   |   |

### October

| S | M | T | W | T | F | S |
|---|---|---|---|---|---|---|
|   |   |   |   |   | 1 | 2 |
| 3 | 4 | 5 | 6 | 7 | 8 | 9 |
| 10 | 11 | 12 | 13 | 14 | 15 | 16 |
| 17 | 18 | 19 | 20 | 21 | 22 | 23 |
| 24 31 | 25 | 26 | 27 | 28 | 29 | 30 |

### November

| S | M | T | W | T | F | S |
|---|---|---|---|---|---|---|
|   | 1 | 2 | 3 | 4 | 5 | 6 |
| 7 | 8 | 9 | 10 | 11 | 12 | 13 |
| 14 | 15 | 16 | 17 | 18 | 19 | 20 |
| 21 | 22 | 23 | 24 | 25 | 26 | 27 |
| 28 | 29 | 30 |   |   |   |   |

### December

| S | M | T | W | T | F | S |
|---|---|---|---|---|---|---|
|   |   |   | 1 | 2 | 3 | 4 |
| 5 | 6 | 7 | 8 | 9 | 10 | 11 |
| 12 | 13 | 14 | 15 | 16 | 17 | 18 |
| 19 | 20 | 21 | 22 | 23 | 24 | 25 |
| 26 | 27 | 28 | 29 | 30 | 31 |   |

Have children cut out the months of the year. Ask them to glue the pictures in order on a sentence strip. Invite them to write the year. You may wish to have children staple the sentence strip to make a headband.

Name _____ Date _____

# Months of the Year Practice

**January**

| S | M | T | W | T | F | S |
|---|---|---|---|---|---|---|
| | | | | | 1 | 2 |
| 3 | 4 | 5 | 6 | 7 | 8 | 9 |
| 10 | 11 | 12 | 13 | 14 | 15 | 16 |
| 17 | 18 | 19 | 20 | 21 | 22 | 23 |
| 24/31 | 25 | 26 | 27 | 28 | 29 | 30 |

**February**

| S | M | T | W | T | F | S |
|---|---|---|---|---|---|---|
| | 1 | 2 | 3 | 4 | 5 | 6 |
| 7 | 8 | 9 | 10 | 11 | 12 | 13 |
| 14 | 15 | 16 | 17 | 18 | 19 | 20 |
| 21 | 22 | 23 | 24 | 25 | 26 | 27 |
| 28 | | | | | | |

**March**

| S | M | T | W | T | F | S |
|---|---|---|---|---|---|---|
| | 1 | 2 | 3 | 4 | 5 | 6 |
| 7 | 8 | 9 | 10 | 11 | 12 | 13 |
| 14 | 15 | 16 | 17 | 18 | 19 | 20 |
| 21 | 22 | 23 | 24 | 25 | 26 | 27 |
| 28 | 29 | 30 | 31 | | | |

**April**

| S | M | T | W | T | F | S |
|---|---|---|---|---|---|---|
| | | | | 1 | 2 | 3 |
| 4 | 5 | 6 | 7 | 8 | 9 | 10 |
| 11 | 12 | 13 | 14 | 15 | 16 | 17 |
| 18 | 19 | 20 | 21 | 22 | 23 | 24 |
| 25 | 26 | 27 | 28 | 29 | 30 | |

**May**

| S | M | T | W | T | F | S |
|---|---|---|---|---|---|---|
| | | | | | | 1 |
| 2 | 3 | 4 | 5 | 6 | 7 | 8 |
| 9 | 10 | 11 | 12 | 13 | 14 | 15 |
| 16 | 17 | 18 | 19 | 20 | 21 | 22 |
| 23/30 | 24/31 | 25 | 26 | 27 | 28 | 29 |

**June**

| S | M | T | W | T | F | S |
|---|---|---|---|---|---|---|
| | | 1 | 2 | 3 | 4 | 5 |
| 6 | 7 | 8 | 9 | 10 | 11 | 12 |
| 13 | 14 | 15 | 16 | 17 | 18 | 19 |
| 20 | 21 | 22 | 23 | 24 | 25 | 26 |
| 27 | 28 | 29 | 30 | | | |

**July**

| S | M | T | W | T | F | S |
|---|---|---|---|---|---|---|
| | | | | 1 | 2 | 3 |
| 4 | 5 | 6 | 7 | 8 | 9 | 10 |
| 11 | 12 | 13 | 14 | 15 | 16 | 17 |
| 18 | 19 | 20 | 21 | 22 | 23 | 24 |
| 25 | 26 | 27 | 28 | 29 | 30 | 31 |

**August**

| S | M | T | W | T | F | S |
|---|---|---|---|---|---|---|
| 1 | 2 | 3 | 4 | 5 | 6 | 7 |
| 8 | 9 | 10 | 11 | 12 | 13 | 14 |
| 15 | 16 | 17 | 18 | 19 | 20 | 21 |
| 22 | 23 | 24 | 25 | 26 | 27 | 28 |
| 29 | 30 | 31 | | | | |

**September**

| S | M | T | W | T | F | S |
|---|---|---|---|---|---|---|
| | | | 1 | 2 | 3 | 4 |
| 5 | 6 | 7 | 8 | 9 | 10 | 11 |
| 12 | 13 | 14 | 15 | 16 | 17 | 18 |
| 19 | 20 | 21 | 22 | 23 | 24 | 25 |
| 26 | 27 | 28 | 29 | 30 | | |

**October**

| S | M | T | W | T | F | S |
|---|---|---|---|---|---|---|
| | | | | | 1 | 2 |
| 3 | 4 | 5 | 6 | 7 | 8 | 9 |
| 10 | 11 | 12 | 13 | 14 | 15 | 16 |
| 17 | 18 | 19 | 20 | 21 | 22 | 23 |
| 24/31 | 25 | 26 | 27 | 28 | 29 | 30 |

**November**

| S | M | T | W | T | F | S |
|---|---|---|---|---|---|---|
| | 1 | 2 | 3 | 4 | 5 | 6 |
| 7 | 8 | 9 | 10 | 11 | 12 | 13 |
| 14 | 15 | 16 | 17 | 18 | 19 | 20 |
| 21 | 22 | 23 | 24 | 25 | 26 | 27 |
| 28 | 29 | 30 | | | | |

**December**

| S | M | T | W | T | F | S |
|---|---|---|---|---|---|---|
| | | | 1 | 2 | 3 | 4 |
| 5 | 6 | 7 | 8 | 9 | 10 | 11 |
| 12 | 13 | 14 | 15 | 16 | 17 | 18 |
| 19 | 20 | 21 | 22 | 23 | 24 | 25 |
| 26 | 27 | 28 | 29 | 30 | 31 | |

**1.** Write the first month of the year.

_____

- - - - - - - - - - - - - - - - - - - - - - - - -

_____

**2.** Write the month that comes after November.

_____

- - - - - - - - - - - - - - - - - - - - - - - - -

_____

**3.** Write your birthday month.

_____

- - - - - - - - - - - - - - - - - - - - - - - - -

_____

**4.** Write the third month of the year.

_____

- - - - - - - - - - - - - - - - - - - - - - - - -

_____

Have children use the calendar to write the name of the correct month on the lines.

Name _____  Date _____

# The Calendar

_____, 20_____

| Sunday | Monday | Tuesday | Wednesday | Thursday | Friday | Saturday |
|--------|--------|---------|-----------|----------|--------|----------|
|        |        |         |           |          |        |          |
|        |        |         |           |          |        |          |
|        |        |         |           |          |        |          |
|        |        |         |           |          |        |          |
|        |        |         |           |          |        |          |

**1.** Write the day of the week on which this month begins.

_____

- - - - - - - - - - - - - - - - - - - - - - - - - -

**2.** Write the day of the week on which this month ends.

_____

- - - - - - - - - - - - - - - - - - - - - - - - - -

**3.** Write the day of the week that is today's date.

_____

- - - - - - - - - - - - - - - - - - - - - - - - - -

Have children write the month and the year. Challenge them to write the numbers on the calendar. You may wish to write the first and last day of the month on the calendar for them. Then, have them look at the calendar and write the days of week indicated.

# Calendar Practice

## April

| Sunday | Monday | Tuesday | Wednesday | Thursday | Friday | Saturday |
|--------|--------|---------|-----------|----------|--------|----------|
|        |        |         | 1         | 2        |        |          |
|        | 6      |         |           |          |        |          |
|        |        |         | 15        |          |        |          |
| 19     |        |         |           |          |        |          |
|        |        |         |           | 30       |        |          |

**1.** How many days are in this month?

28          30

**2.** How many Mondays are in this month?

two          four

**3.** What is the date of the first Saturday?

April 4          April 20

**4.** On what day is April 7?

Friday          Tuesday

Have children write the missing numbers on the calendar. Then, have them circle the answers to the questions.

Name _____    Date _____

# Find Birthdays on the Calendar

### January

| S | M | T | W | T | F | S |
|---|---|---|---|---|---|---|
|   |   |   |   |   | 1 | 2 |
| 3 | 4 | 5 | 6 | 7 | 8 | 9 |
| 10 | 11 | 12 | 13 | 14 | 15 | 16 |
| 17 | 18 | 19 | 20 | 21 | 22 | 23 |
| 24 31 | 25 | 26 | 27 | 28 | 29 | 30 |

### February

| S | M | T | W | T | F | S |
|---|---|---|---|---|---|---|
|   | 1 | 2 | 3 | 4 | 5 | 6 |
| 7 | 8 | 9 | 10 | 11 | 12 | 13 |
| 14 | 15 | 16 | 17 | 18 | 19 | 20 |
| 21 | 22 | 23 | 24 | 25 | 26 | 27 |
| 28 |   |   |   |   |   |   |

### March

| S | M | T | W | T | F | S |
|---|---|---|---|---|---|---|
|   | 1 | 2 | 3 | 4 | 5 | 6 |
| 7 | 8 | 9 | 10 | 11 | 12 | 13 |
| 14 | 15 | 16 | 17 | 18 | 19 | 20 |
| 21 | 22 | 23 | 24 | 25 | 26 | 27 |
| 28 | 29 | 30 | 31 |   |   |   |

### April

| S | M | T | W | T | F | S |
|---|---|---|---|---|---|---|
|   |   |   |   | 1 | 2 | 3 |
| 4 | 5 | 6 | 7 | 8 | 9 | 10 |
| 11 | 12 | 13 | 14 | 15 | 16 | 17 |
| 18 | 19 | 20 | 21 | 22 | 23 | 24 |
| 25 | 26 | 27 | 28 | 29 | 30 |   |

### May

| S | M | T | W | T | F | S |
|---|---|---|---|---|---|---|
|   |   |   |   |   |   | 1 |
| 2 | 3 | 4 | 5 | 6 | 7 | 8 |
| 9 | 10 | 11 | 12 | 13 | 14 | 15 |
| 16 | 17 | 18 | 19 | 20 | 21 | 22 |
| 23 30 | 24 31 | 25 | 26 | 27 | 28 | 29 |

### June

| S | M | T | W | T | F | S |
|---|---|---|---|---|---|---|
|   |   | 1 | 2 | 3 | 4 | 5 |
| 6 | 7 | 8 | 9 | 10 | 11 | 12 |
| 13 | 14 | 15 | 16 | 17 | 18 | 19 |
| 20 | 21 | 22 | 23 | 24 | 25 | 26 |
| 27 | 28 | 29 | 30 |   |   |   |

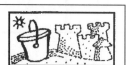

### July

| S | M | T | W | T | F | S |
|---|---|---|---|---|---|---|
|   |   |   |   | 1 | 2 | 3 |
| 4 | 5 | 6 | 7 | 8 | 9 | 10 |
| 11 | 12 | 13 | 14 | 15 | 16 | 17 |
| 18 | 19 | 20 | 21 | 22 | 23 | 24 |
| 25 | 26 | 27 | 28 | 29 | 30 | 31 |

### August

| S | M | T | W | T | F | S |
|---|---|---|---|---|---|---|
| 1 | 2 | 3 | 4 | 5 | 6 | 7 |
| 8 | 9 | 10 | 11 | 12 | 13 | 14 |
| 15 | 16 | 17 | 18 | 19 | 20 | 21 |
| 22 | 23 | 24 | 25 | 26 | 27 | 28 |
| 29 | 30 | 31 |   |   |   |   |

### September

| S | M | T | W | T | F | S |
|---|---|---|---|---|---|---|
|   |   |   | 1 | 2 | 3 | 4 |
| 5 | 6 | 7 | 8 | 9 | 10 | 11 |
| 12 | 13 | 14 | 15 | 16 | 17 | 18 |
| 19 | 20 | 21 | 22 | 23 | 24 | 25 |
| 26 | 27 | 28 | 29 | 30 |   |   |

### October

| S | M | T | W | T | F | S |
|---|---|---|---|---|---|---|
|   |   |   |   |   | 1 | 2 |
| 3 | 4 | 5 | 6 | 7 | 8 | 9 |
| 10 | 11 | 12 | 13 | 14 | 15 | 16 |
| 17 | 18 | 19 | 20 | 21 | 22 | 23 |
| 24 31 | 25 | 26 | 27 | 28 | 29 | 30 |

### November

| S | M | T | W | T | F | S |
|---|---|---|---|---|---|---|
|   | 1 | 2 | 3 | 4 | 5 | 6 |
| 7 | 8 | 9 | 10 | 11 | 12 | 13 |
| 14 | 15 | 16 | 17 | 18 | 19 | 20 |
| 21 | 22 | 23 | 24 | 25 | 26 | 27 |
| 28 | 29 | 30 |   |   |   |   |

### December

| S | M | T | W | T | F | S |
|---|---|---|---|---|---|---|
|   |   |   | 1 | 2 | 3 | 4 |
| 5 | 6 | 7 | 8 | 9 | 10 | 11 |
| 12 | 13 | 14 | 15 | 16 | 17 | 18 |
| 19 | 20 | 21 | 22 | 23 | 24 | 25 |
| 26 | 27 | 28 | 29 | 30 | 31 |   |

## My birthday is in _____ .

Have children write the month of their birthday. Ask them to color their birthday month red. Have them color the month before their birthday green. Invite them to color the month after their birthday blue. You may wish to have children find a friend's birthday on the calendar and count how many months apart their friend's birthday is from their own.

**Unit 1: Calendar Readiness**
Cool Calendar Skills K-1, SV 7099-8

# Find the Birthdays

| Sunday | Monday | Tuesday | Wednesday | Thursday | Friday | Saturday |
|--------|--------|---------|-----------|----------|--------|----------|
|        |        |         | 1         | 2        | 3      | 4        |
| 5      | 6      | 7       | 8         | 9        | 10     | 11       |
| 12     | 13     | 14      | 15        | 16       | 17     | 18       |
| 19     | 20     | 21      | 22        | 23       | 24     | 25       |
| 26     | 27     | 28      | 29        | 30       |        |          |

**1.** Kasi's birthday is on the first day of the month.

**2.** Maria's birthday is on the second Friday of the month.

**3.** Barry's birthday is two days after Maria's birthday.

**4.** Jacob's birthday is on the fourth Tuesday of the month.

Have children find the dates of the children's birthdays. Then, ask them to write their names on the date of their birthday on the calendar.

# Graph Birthdays

| January | _ _ _ _ _ _ _ | July | _ _ _ _ _ _ _ |
|---|---|---|---|
| February | _ _ _ _ _ _ _ | August | _ _ _ _ _ _ _ |
| March | _ _ _ _ _ _ _ | September | _ _ _ _ _ _ _ |
| April | _ _ _ _ _ _ _ | October | _ _ _ _ _ _ _ |
| May | _ _ _ _ _ _ _ | November | _ _ _ _ _ _ _ |
| June | _ _ _ _ _ _ _ | December | _ _ _ _ _ _ _ |

Make a large graph and hang it on the wall. Make a column for each month of the year and write the names of the months on the graph. Invite children to write their name on a piece of paper and tape it on the graph above their birthday month.  Have children look at the graph and write how many birthdays are in each month of the year. You may wish to have them find the months with the most and the fewest birthdays.

# August

| Sunday | Monday | Tuesday | Wednesday | Thursday | Friday | Saturday |
|--------|--------|---------|-----------|----------|--------|----------|
|        |        |         |           |          |        |          |
|        |        |         |           |          |        |          |
|        |        |         |           |          |        |          |
|        |        |         |           |          |        |          |
|        |        |         |           |          |        |          |

**1.** Write the number of days in August.

_____

**2.** Write the date of the second Tuesday.

_____

**3.** Write the date of Friendship Day.

_____

**4.** Write the date of National Watermelon Day.

_____

Have children write the numbers on the calendar. You may wish to write in the first day of the month for them. Discuss Friendship Day on the first Sunday in August and National Watermelon Day on August 3.

Name _____  Date _____

# Friendship Day

Friendship Day is on _____

_____.

Discuss with children that Friendship Day is the first Sunday in August. Encourage them to look at the class calendar to find the date and write it. Have children write "My Friends" in the first box. Ask them to draw pictures of three friends in the remaining boxes. Then, have children cut out the boxes. You may wish to have them string the pictures on yarn to make a friendship necklace.

Name _____ Date _____

# Watermelon Day

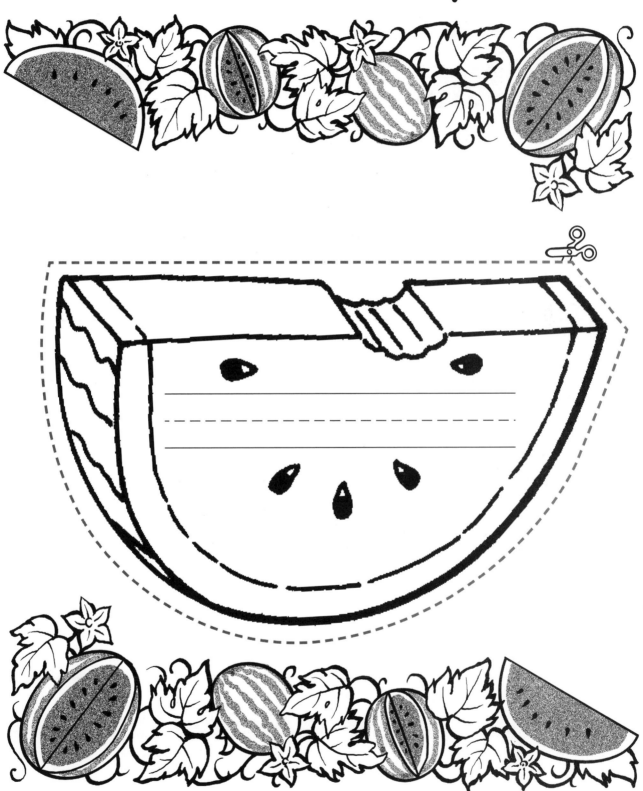

Discuss with children that National Watermelon Day is on August 3. Have them write the date on the picture of the watermelon and color it. Invite children to cut it out and glue it on a sentence strip. Then have them staple it to make a headband. You may wish to have them wear the headband and serve watermelon slices for snack.

# September

| Sunday | Monday | Tuesday | Wednesday | Thursday | Friday | Saturday |
|--------|--------|---------|-----------|----------|--------|----------|
|        |        |         |           |          |        |          |
|        |        |         |           |          |        |          |
|        |        |         |           |          |        |          |
|        |        |         |           |          |        |          |
|        |        |         |           |          |        |          |

**1.** Color Labor Day's date red.

**2.** Color the date of Grandparent's Day blue.

**3.** Color the first day of fall orange.

Have children write the numbers on the calendar. You may wish to write in the first day of the month for them. Discuss Labor Day (first Monday in September), Grandparent's Day (first Sunday after Labor Day), and fall (September 22 or 23). Encourage them to color the dates on the calendar.

# Grandparent's Day

Grandparent's Day is the first Sunday after Labor Day. It is on

_____

_____.

_____

Juan's birthday is on _____.

Have children look at the class calendar to find the date of Grandparent's Day and write it. Tell children that Juan's birthday is in this month. It is three days after Grandparent's Day. Challenge them to refer to the class calendar and write the date of Juan's birthday. Have them draw a picture of grandparents.

Name _____   Date _____

# Fall Happenings

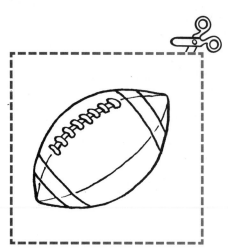

Discuss with children the season of fall. Have them cut out and glue in the boxes the pictures of things they might see in the fall.

# October

| Sunday | Monday | Tuesday | Wednesday | Thursday | Friday | Saturday |
|--------|--------|---------|-----------|----------|--------|----------|
|        |        |         |           |          |        |          |
|        |        |         |           |          |        |          |
|        |        |         |           |          |        |          |
|        |        |         |           |          |        |          |
|        |        |         |           |          |        |          |

**1.** Write the numbers on the calendar.

**2.** Circle the name of the month in orange.

**3.** Color the days of the week red.

**4.** Color the number of today's date green.

Have children write the numbers on the calendar. You may wish to write in the first day of the month for them. Have them color the calendar as indicated.

# Columbus Day

In 1492, Columbus sailed the ocean blue.
Columbus Day is on

_____

– – – – – – – – – – – – – – – – – – – – – – – – – –

_____ .

Discuss with children Columbus Day (second Monday in October). Have children write the month and date. Ask them to draw Columbus' ship.

# Growing Pumpkins

**1.**

October 31

**2.**

October 20

**3.**

October 1

Discuss with children how pumpkins grow. Have them draw a line from each picture that shows how much the pumpkin vine has grown on each date. You may wish to have children color the pictures and draw a face on the large pumpkin.

# November

| Sunday | Monday | Tuesday | Wednesday | Thursday | Friday | Saturday |
|--------|--------|---------|-----------|----------|--------|----------|
|        |        |         |           |          |        |          |
|        |        |         |           |          |        |          |
|        |        |         |           |          |        |          |
|        |        |         |           |          |        |          |
|        |        |         |           |          |        |          |

**1.** Election Day is the second Tuesday. _____

**2.** Veteran's Day is _____.

**3.** Thanksgiving is the fourth Thursday. _____

Discuss with children Election Day (second Tuesday in November), Veteran's Day (November 11), and Thanksgiving (fourth Thursday in November). Have children write the numbers on the calendar. You may wish to write in the first day of the month for them. Challenge children to write the dates of the special days in November.

# Pilgrims on the Mayflower

| September | | | | | | |
|---|---|---|---|---|---|---|
| S | M | T | W | T | F | S |
|  |  | 1 | 2 | 3 | 4 | 5 |
| 6 | 7 | 8 | 9 | 10 | 11 | 12 |
| 13 | 14 | 15 | 16 | 17 | 18 | 19 |
| 20 | 21 | 22 | 23 | 24 | 25 | 26 |
| 27 | 28 | 29 | 30 |  |  |  |

| October | | | | | | |
|---|---|---|---|---|---|---|
| S | M | T | W | T | F | S |
|  |  |  |  | 1 | 2 | 3 |
| 4 | 5 | 6 | 7 | 8 | 9 | 10 |
| 11 | 12 | 13 | 14 | 15 | 16 | 17 |
| 18 | 19 | 20 | 21 | 22 | 23 | 24 |
| 25 | 26 | 27 | 28 | 29 | 30 | 31 |

| November | | | | | | |
|---|---|---|---|---|---|---|
| S | M | T | W | T | F | S |
| 1 | 2 | 3 | 4 | 5 | 6 | 7 |
| 8 | 9 | 10 | 11 | 12 | 13 | 14 |
| 15 | 16 | 17 | 18 | 19 | 20 | 21 |
| 22 | 23 | 24 | 25 | 26 | 27 | 28 |
| 29 | 30 |  |  |  |  |  |

**1.** The Mayflower left England on September 6, 1620. Color the date red.

**2.** The Mayflower landed in America on November 11, 1620. Color the date green.

**3.** Count how many days the Pilgrims were on the _____ ship. Write the number. _____

Have children use the calendars to count how many days it took the Mayflower to reach America. You may wish to have children locate England and America on a map. Discuss with children the difficulties the Pilgrims had while on the ship.

# The First Thanksgiving

| | |
|---|---|
| Food the Pilgrims had on Thanksgiving. | Food my family has on Thanksgiving. |

Thanksgiving is on the fourth

_ _ _ _ _ _ _ _ _ _ _ _ _ _ _ _ _ _

of November.

The Pilgrims celebrated for three days. Write the day of the week that was the end of their celebration.

_ _ _ _ _ _ _ _ _ _ _ _ _ _ _ _ _ _

Discuss with children the types of food that the Pilgrims had on the first Thanksgiving. Have them draw pictures of the foods the Pilgrims might have had and the foods that their families have. Encourage children to write the day of the week on which Thanksgiving is celebrated and the day of the week that the Pilgrims ended their celebration.

# December

| Sunday | Monday | Tuesday | Wednesday | Thursday | Friday | Saturday |
|--------|--------|---------|-----------|----------|--------|----------|
|        |        |         |           |          |        |          |
|        |        |         |           |          |        |          |
|        |        |         |           |          |        |          |
|        |        |         |           |          |        |          |
|        |        |         |           |          |        |          |

**1.** Circle the number that comes after 10.

**2.** Color the numbers that come between 28 and 31 red.

**3.** Color the number that is two before 19.

**4.** Circle the number that is the same as today's date.

Have children write the numbers on the calendar. You may wish to discuss Hanukkah, Kwanzaa, and Christmas. Have children follow the directions above.

# Holiday Preparations

## 1. Mail the cards on December 9.

_____
- - - - - - - - - - - - - - - - - - - - - - -
_____

## 2. Put up decorations on December 11.

_____
- - - - - - - - - - - - - - - - - - - - - - -
_____

## 3. Buy the gifts on December 14.

_____
- - - - - - - - - - - - - - - - - - - - - - -
_____

## 4. Bake cookies on December 22.

_____
- - - - - - - - - - - - - - - - - - - - - - -
_____

Discuss with children things that people do to prepare for the holidays. Invite them to look at the class calendar and find the days of the week on which these dates fall. Have children write the days and color the pictures.

# Winter Happenings

Discuss with children the season of winter. Have them cut out and glue in the boxes the pictures of things they might see in the winter.

# January

| Sunday | Monday | Tuesday | Wednesday | Thursday | Friday | Saturday |
|--------|--------|---------|-----------|----------|--------|----------|
|        |        |         |           |          |        |          |
|        |        |         |           |          |        |          |
|        |        |         |           |          |        |          |
|        |        |         |           |          |        |          |
|        |        |         |           |          |        |          |

1. Draw a triangle on New Year's Day.

2. Draw a star on Martin Luther King, Jr.'s birthday.

3. Color all of the days in a green, yellow, red pattern.

Discuss with children New Year's Day (January 1) and Martin Luther King, Jr.'s birthday (January 15). Have children write the numbers on the calendar. Invite them to draw shapes on the special days and color the days of the month in a pattern.

# Snowman Sequencing

### Saturday

### Sunday

### Monday

Have children cut out the pictures of the snowman. Then have them glue the pictures in the box that shows what the snowman would look like on each day of the week as it melted.

Name _____ Date _____

# Martin Luther King, Jr.

## Martin Luther King, Jr.'s birthday is on

_____

- - - - - - - - - - - - - - - - - - - - - - - - - - - - - - - -

_____ .

Discuss with children Martin Luther King, Jr.'s life and the importance of his "I Have a Dream" speech given on August 28, 1963. Have children write his birth date (January 15). Invite them to draw a picture that shows their dream of what might make the world a better place in which to live.

# February

| Sunday | Monday | Tuesday | Wednesday | Thursday | Friday | Saturday |
|---|---|---|---|---|---|---|
| | | | | | | |
| | | | | | | |
| | | | | | | |
| | | | | | | |
| | | | | | | |

**1.** Color Groundhog Day green.

**2.** Color Valentine's Day red.

**3.** Color Presidents' Day blue.

Discuss with the children Groundhog Day (Feb. 2), Valentine's Day (Feb. 14), and Presidents' Day (third Monday in Feb.). Have children write the numbers on the calendar. You may wish to have the children color Abraham Lincoln's birthday (Feb. 12) and George Washington's birthday (Feb. 22).

Name _____  Date _____

# Groundhog Day

Groundhog Day is on

_____

— — — — — — — — — — — — — — — —

_____ .

Have the children sing the groundhog song on page 5. Have children write the month and the date (February 2). Ask them to color the groundhog and draw his shadow.

# Valentine's Day

February 23

February 14

February 6

February 28

Have children decorate the heart that has the date of Valentine's Day (February 14). Ask them to fold construction paper into fourths. Invite them to cut out the hearts and glue them in order on the construction paper.

# March

| Sunday | Monday | Tuesday | Wednesday | Thursday | Friday | Saturday |
|--------|--------|---------|-----------|----------|--------|----------|
|        |        |         |           |          |        |          |
|        |        |         |           |          |        |          |
|        |        |         |           |          |        |          |
|        |        |         |           |          |        |          |
|        |        |         |           |          |        |          |

**1.** Color St. Patrick's Day green.

**2.** Color the first day of spring yellow.

**3.** Count by 5's. Color every fifth number blue.

Discuss with children St. Patrick's Day (March 17) and spring (March 20 or 21). Have them write the numbers on the calendar. Ask children to count by 5's and follow the directions above.

# St. Patrick's Day

St. Patrick's Day is on March 17.

**1.** Write the day of the week of St. Patrick's Day on the top line.

**2.** Write the date of St. Patrick's Day on the second line.

Discuss with children St. Patrick's Day (March 17). Have them color and cut out the shamrock after they write the dates. You may wish to have them glue the shamrock on a sentence strip and staple it to make a headband.

# Spring Happenings

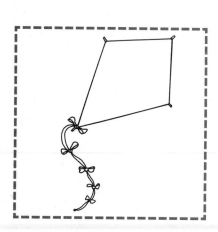

Discuss with children the season of spring. Have them cut out and glue in the boxes the pictures of things they might see in the spring.

# April

| Sunday | Monday | Tuesday | Wednesday | Thursday | Friday | Saturday |
|--------|--------|---------|-----------|----------|--------|----------|
|        |        |         |           |          |        |          |
|        |        |         |           |          |        |          |
|        |        |         |           |          |        |          |
|        |        |         |           |          |        |          |
|        |        |         |           |          |        |          |

**1.** Draw a picture of the earth on Earth Day.

**2.** Color the first Tuesday and the first Thursday green.

**3.** Color all two-digit numbers blue.

Discuss with children Earth Day (April 22). Have children write the numbers on the calendar. Have them follow the directions above.

# Earth Day

Earth Day is April 22.

Earth Day is _____.

Discuss Earth Day (April 22) with children. Ask children to write the date and color the picture. Then have them cut out the box. Invite children to glue the picture on a small brown sack. You may wish to have them walk around the school and fill their bags with litter.

# Baby Chicks in Spring

## April

| Sunday | Monday | Tuesday | Wednesday | Thursday | Friday | Saturday |
|--------|--------|---------|-----------|----------|--------|----------|
| 1 | 2 | 3 | 4 | 5 | 6 | |
| 7 | 8 | 9 | 10 | 11 | 12 | 13 |
| 14 | 15 | 16 | 17 | 18 | 19 | 20 |
| 21 | 22 | 23 | 24 | 25 | 26 | 27 |
| 28 | 29 | 30 | | | | |

**1.** The mother hen laid 3 eggs on April 3.
Color the date green.

**2.** The eggs will hatch in 21 days.
Find the date that the chicks will hatch.
Color the date yellow.

**3.** Draw a picture of the baby chicks.

Have children color the dates on the calendar. Ask them to draw a picture of the baby chicks.

# May

| Sunday | Monday | Tuesday | Wednesday | Thursday | Friday | Saturday |
|--------|--------|---------|-----------|----------|--------|----------|
|        |        |         |           |          |        |          |
|        |        |         |           |          |        |          |
|        |        |         |           |          |        |          |
|        |        |         |           |          |        |          |
|        |        |         |           |          |        |          |

**1.** Color the days between the 6th and the 10th green.

**2.** Draw a circle on Cinco de Mayo.

**3.** Draw a heart on Mother's Day.

**4.** Count by 10's. Color every 10th number yellow.

Discuss with children Cinco de Mayo (May 5) and Mother's Day (second Sunday in May). Have children write the numbers on the calendar. Ask them to count by 10's and follow the directions above.

# Cinco de Mayo

Cinco de Mayo is on  _____
- - - - - - - - - - - - - - - - - - - - - - -
_____ .

piñata

flag of Mexico

Discuss Cinco de Mayo (May 5) with children. Have children color the pictures and write the date of Cinco de Mayo. Then have them cut out the four boxes and glue them upside down on the sides of an empty milk carton. Have children place a few beans inside the carton, add a craft stick to the opening, and staple closed. Invite them to use it as a maraca.

Name _____    Date _____

# Mother's Day

Mother's Day is the second Sunday in May.

_____

The date is _____ .

Have children look at the class calendar and write the date of Mother's Day (second Sunday in May). Ask them to decorate the picture and cut it out. Invite them to fold a piece of construction paper in half and glue the picture on the front to make a Mother's Day card.

Name _____    Date _____

# June

| Sunday | Monday | Tuesday | Wednesday | Thursday | Friday | Saturday |
|--------|--------|---------|-----------|----------|--------|----------|
|        |        |         |           |          |        |          |
|        |        |         |           |          |        |          |
|        |        |         |           |          |        |          |
|        |        |         |           |          |        |          |
|        |        |         |           |          |        |          |

**1.** Color the even numbers orange.

**2.** Color the odd numbers blue.

**3.** Draw a star on Flag Day.

**4.** Draw a triangle on Father's Day.

Discuss with children Flag Day (June 14) and Father's Day (third Sunday in June). Have children write the numbers on the calendar. You may wish to teach a lesson on odd and even numbers. Have children follow the directions above.

Name _____     Date _____

# Father's Day

Father's Day is the third Sunday in June.

_____

The date is _____ .

Have children look at the class calendar and write the date of Father's Day (third Sunday in June). Ask them to decorate the picture and cut it out. Invite them to fold a piece of construction paper in half and glue the picture on the front to make a Father's Day card.

# Summer Happenings

Discuss with children the season of summer. Have them cut out and glue in the boxes the pictures of things they might see in the summer.

# July

| Sunday | Monday | Tuesday | Wednesday | Thursday | Friday | Saturday |
|--------|--------|---------|-----------|----------|--------|----------|
|        |        |         |           |          |        |          |
|        |        |         |           |          |        |          |
|        |        |         |           |          |        |          |
|        |        |         |           |          |        |          |
|        |        |         |           |          |        |          |

**1.** Draw a star on July 4th.

**2.** Draw a moon on July 20th for Moon Day.

**3.** Color the third Sunday yellow for National Ice Cream Day.

**4.** Color the first, third, and fifth weeks red.

Discuss Independence Day with children. Have children write the numbers on the calendar. Challenge children to find information on Moon Day and National Ice Cream Day. You may wish to talk about ordinal numbers with children. Have them follow the directions above.

# Independence Day

_____

- - - - - - - - - - - - - - - -

In _____ the United States
flew the first flag.

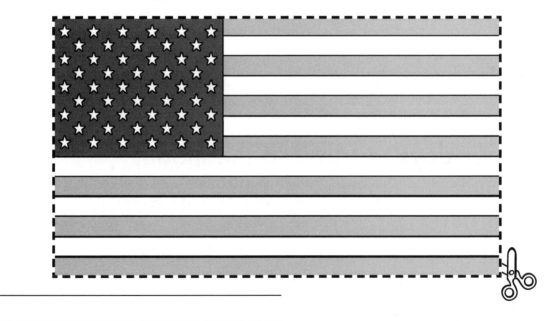

_____

- - - - - - - - - - - - - - - -

In _____ the United States
flies this flag.

Discuss with children Independence Day and the meaning of the symbols on the flag. Challenge children to write the year 1777 and the current year. Have children color and cut out the flags. You may wish to have them glue the flags on craft sticks and use them in a Fourth of July parade.

Name _____    Date _____

# Moon Day

Moon Day is on July 20.

It took four days to travel to the moon.

**1.** Write the date the astronauts left earth.

_____

- - - - - - - - - - - - - - - - - - - - - - - - - - - - - -

_____

**2.** Write the date the astronauts returned.

_____

- - - - - - - - - - - - - - - - - - - - - - - - - - - - - -

_____

Discuss with children the first landing on the moon that took place July 20, 1969. Have them look at the class calendar and write the date the astronauts left and the date they returned. Invite children to color the astronaut and draw his footprints on the moon.

# Answer Key

**page 7**
**1.** 1, 3, 2  **2.** 1, 3, 2  **3.** 3, 1, 2

**page 8**
**1.** 4, 2, 1, 3  **2.** 3, 4, 1, 2

**page 9**
Drawings will vary.

**page 10**
Fall: tree and leaves; Winter: penguin; Spring: flowers; Summer: pail

**page 11**
March: shamrock; April: Earth; May: Mother's Day card

**page 12**
June: father; July: U.S. flag; August: watermelon

**page 13**
September: grandparent; October: ship; November: turkey

**page 14**
December: tree; January: Happy New Year baby; February: Valentine's heart

**page 15**
Sunday, Monday, Tuesday, Wednesday, Thursday, Friday, Saturday

**page 16**
**1.** Sunday—sun or seal  **2.** Monday—mouse  **3.** Tuesday—top  **4.** Wednesday—wagon  **5.** Thursday—thumb  **6.** Friday—fish  **7.** Saturday—sun or seal

**page 17**
Answers and drawings will vary.

**page 18**
Sunday, Monday, Tuesday, Wednesday, Thursday, Friday, Saturday; Tuesdays—blue

**page 19**
January, February, March, April, May, June, July, August, September, October, November, December

**page 20**
January, February, March, April, May, June, July, August, September, October, November, December

**page 21**
**1.** January  **2.** December  **3.** Answers will vary.  **4.** March

**page 22**
Check answers based on current month.

**page 23**
Check calendars.  **1.** 30  **2.** four  **3.** April 4  **4.** Tuesday

**page 24**
Answers will vary.

**page 25**
**1.** 1  **2.** 10  **3.** 12  **4.** 28

**page 26**
Check answers based on graph.

**page 27**
**1.** 31  **2.–3.** Check answers based on current month.  **4.** August 3

**page 28**
Answer and drawings will vary.

**page 29**
August 3

**page 30**
Check answers based on current month.

**page 31**
Check answers based on current month.

**page 32**
apple, football, school bus. Order may vary.

**page 33**
**1.** 1 through 31  **2.** October  **3.** Sunday, Monday, Tuesday, Wednesday, Thursday, Friday, Saturday  **4.** Check answers based on current month.

**page 34**
Check answers based on current month.

**page 35**
**1.** October 1 **2.** October 20 **3.** October 31

**page 36**
**1.** Check answer based on current month.
**2.** November 11 **3.** Check answer based on current month.

**page 37**
**1.–2.** Check calendars. **3.** 67

**page 38**
Drawings will vary. Thursday; Saturday

**page 39**
**1.** 11 **2.** 29, 30 **3.** 17 **4.** Check answers.

**page 40**
Check answers based on current month.

**page 41**
snowman, Happy New Year baby, tree with no leaves. Order may vary.

**page 42**
**1.** January 1 **2.** January 15 **3.** Check calendars for pattern.

**page 43**
Saturday: full snowman; Sunday: partially melted snowman; Monday: entirely melted

**page 44**
January 15. Drawings will vary.

**page 45**
Check calendars based on current month.

**page 46**
February 2. Check drawings.

**page 47**
February 6, February 14, February 23, February 28

**page 48**
**1.** March 17 **2.** March 20 or 21, based on current year **3.** Check calendars.

**page 49**
**1.** Check answer based on current month.
**2.** March 17, current year

**page 50**
kite, butterfly, flower. Order may vary.

**page 51**
**1.** April 22: picture of earth **2.–3.** Check calendars.

**page 52**
April 22

**page 53**
April 3: green; April 24: yellow. Drawings will vary.

**page 54**
**1.** Color 7, 8, and 9 green. **2.** Circle May 5. **3.** Draw a heart on Mother's Day. **4.** Check calendars for yellow.

**page 55**
May 5

**page 56**
Check answer based on current month.

**page 57**
Check calendars.

**page 58**
Check answer based on current month.

**page 59**
sandcastle, swimming pool, butterfly. Order may vary.

**page 60**
Check calendars.

**page 61**
1777. Answer should be current year.

**page 62**
**1.** July 16 **2.** July 24. Drawings will vary.